TEAM SPIRIT

Get in the Game with 11 Sports-Inspired Quilts

Suzzie Schuyler

Team Spirit: Get in the Game with 11 Sports-Inspired Quilts
© 2015 by Suzzie Schuyler

Martingale®
19021 120th Ave. NE, Ste. 102
Bothell, WA 98011-9511 USA
ShopMartingale.com

No part of this product may be reproduced in any form, unless otherwise stated, in which case reproduction is limited to the use of the purchaser. The written instructions, photographs, designs, projects, and patterns are intended for the personal, noncommercial use of the retail purchaser and are under federal copyright laws; they are not to be reproduced by any electronic, mechanical, or other means, including informational storage or retrieval systems, for commercial use. Permission is granted to photocopy patterns for the personal use of the retail purchaser. Attention teachers: Martingale encourages you to use this book for teaching, subject to the restrictions stated above.

The information in this book is presented in good faith, but no warranty is given nor results guaranteed. Since Martingale has no control over choice of materials or procedures, the company assumes no responsibility for the use of this information.

Printed in China

20 19 18 17 16 15   8 7 6 5 4 3 2 1

Library of Congress Cataloging-in-Publication Data is available upon request.

ISBN: 978-1-60468-672-2

Mission Statement

Dedicated to providing quality products and service to inspire creativity.

Credits

PUBLISHER AND CHIEF VISIONARY OFFICER
Jennifer Erbe Keltner

EDITORIAL DIRECTOR
Karen Costello Soltys

DESIGN DIRECTOR
Paula Schlosser

ACQUISITIONS EDITOR
Karen M. Burns

PRODUCTION MANAGER
Regina Girard

TECHNICAL EDITOR
Monique Dillard

COVER AND INTERIOR DESIGNER
Connor Chin

COPY EDITOR
Sheila Chapman Ryan

PHOTOGRAPHER
Brent Kane

ILLUSTRATOR
Missy Shepler

Contents

Introduction 5
Tools of the Trade 6
Working with Sports-Theme Prints 7
Tips for Easy Piecing 10
Binding 10
Alternate Colorways 12

THE PROJECTS

Start Your Engines 14
Season Tickets 16
Pregame Warm-Up 20
Starting Time 23
Halftime Event 26
Friday Night Lights 30
Go Team! 34
Game Delay 37
The Winning Strategy 40
Going For Overtime 43
Tailgating Table Runner 46

About the Author 48
Acknowledgments 48

Introduction

So many quilters these days are sports fans—or they live with one or are getting ready to send their favorite fan off to college. I've heard from many quilters who want to emphasize the popular sport-logo fabrics in their quilts.

Who are the biggest sports fanatics in your life? I bet they need a new favorite quilt to show their team colors. But where do you begin? That's where this book comes in!

I've created a variety of designs that will let you use these sport-logo fabrics (or any novelty print, really) to their best advantage. To bring these specialty fabrics to the forefront, you'll find that tone-on-tone prints make great backgrounds and accent fabrics. The correct background, combined with patterns designed specifically to showcase the focus fabrics, is just what you need to make the ultimate sporty quilt.

My goal is to provide you with options for using sporty fabric no matter the size of the design on the print, and to help you to make the quilts uniquely your own. I know you've seen these sports-related fabrics on display, and you'd love to make a quilt using them. I hope this book will help you see specialty theme fabrics in a different way, get your creative juices going, and provide more ideas for using these fun fabrics. Most of all I want you to be inspired.

—Suzzie

Tools of the Trade

Before you get started, make sure you have all the tools and supplies you'll need to be successful with your sports-themed quilts. I have a go-to list of products I use, and while you can get away with having fewer rulers or may not need a tool for making triangles, it's nice to add these items to your sewing tool kit as you can.

WHAT YOU'LL NEED

- Sewing machine in good working order
- ¼" and open-toe presser feet
- Walking foot or dual-feed option on your sewing machine for stitching the binding
- Cotton or poly-cotton thread in a neutral color such as gray or tan for piecing
- Rotary cutter with new blade and self-healing cutting mat
- Acrylic rulers: 6½ x 24" with 45° marking; 9½" square; 4½" square with a diagonal line; 6" square with a diagonal line
- Optional: specialty rulers or tool for making half-square triangles, such as the Angler 2 or Easy Angle
- Marking pen/pencil for fabric
- Spray sizing for taming bias edges
- Fork or double pins for pinning multiple intersecting seams
- Post-It notes for marking an accurate ¼" seam allowance on your machine
- Thread snips or small scissors for trimming threads
- Florescent tape for marking cutting lines on acrylic rulers
- Optional: Chocolate and your favorite music!

Sewing Machine

If you own multiple sewing machines, make sure you use the same machine for the entire quilt project. Not only is there a variance between the ¼" seam allowance on sewing machines, but the stitch lengths can also vary.

BEFORE STARTING

Below is my basic list of things to keep in mind for any of the projects in this book.

- All seams are sewn with ¼"-wide seam allowances.
- Press all the seam allowances toward the darker fabric unless instructed otherwise.
- Yardage is based on 42"-wide fabric.
- Lay out the blocks before sewing them together so you can stitch them in the correct order.
- Read all the directions before starting.
- Have fun!

Working with Sports-Theme Prints

As for any novelty print, it pays to keep a few things in mind when working with sports prints to make sure your quilt turns out exactly as you want it. From selecting fabrics to cutting them, let's go over some pointers.

- **Depending on the size of the logo** or motif, more fabric may be required than what's in the materials list (especially for the quilts cut on a 45° angle) when your fabric has a large design. Logos that are 2" to 4" across work well with the yardage listed in these projects. If you use large-scale logos, such as ones that are 6" or wider across, you may need to buy more yardage. You also need to look at how close together the logos are printed. If there's lots of background color between each logo, you may need more yardage to accommodate the number of logo squares or rectangles you need to cut for the quilt.

- **Using tone-on-tone prints** for coordinating fabrics is the secret to showcasing the sports fabrics. Depending on the quilt pattern you're making, you'll need two or three of these fabrics for background. They read as solid from a distance, but add a quiet dimension and a bit more interest than ordinary solids.

- **Sometimes solid fabrics** can be integrated with the tone-on-tone prints. Notice in "Friday Night Lights" (page 30) that the black solid blends into the same black used in the border, creating the illusion of a unique border. This is a good example of how color can change the look of the design. The red is a tone-on-tone, adding subtle interest. I recommend using no more than one solid, and then selecting coordinating tone on tones for the other background fabrics.

- **When using multiple sport prints** in the quilt, try to select background fabrics that not only coordinate with the focus fabrics but *also* contrast with these fabrics. For example, see both the black and white prints used in "Pregame Warm-Up" (page 20); both fabrics coordinate *and* contrast in this quilt.

FUSSY CUTTING

Fussy cutting is a term used to describe selectively cutting a particular section of the fabric, such as a motif, print, wording, or panel, so that the design can be centered on the finished block. I generally use one of two different methods for fussy cutting theme prints, depending on the size of the design.

For smaller, continuous designs, place the appropriate-sized ruler over the motif on the fabric, which is laid out with the right side facing you. Move the ruler over the fabric until the motif is centered in the strip width needed (a ¼" seam allowance is included in the measurements given), and then rotary cut the strip. Crosscut the strips in the same way when you're cutting squares or rectangles from the strips.

Florescent Tape

Here's where the florescent tape I mentioned (page 6) comes in handy. I like to use it to mark the line on the ruler that corresponds to my strip width so I can see at a glance what part of the motifs will be visible in my cut fabric strips. For example, if you need 4½" squares, place the tape along the 4½" line on your ruler so that you can easily place that line along the edge of your fabric. Everything from that line to the edge of your ruler will be part of your 4½"-wide strip. If you don't like where the motifs fall, trim off some fabric from the edge and move the ruler over.

The other method I use for fussy cutting is to cut a plastic template the needed size plus a ¼" seam allowance. Mark the center of the template with crosshairs so it's easier to center the motif. Center the template over the design and rotary cut around the template carefully. You may want to use a chalk marker and draw lines around the template first, and then remove the template and cut each side with the ruler.

Center template over desired area of print.

CUTTING ON THE DIAGONAL

This cutting method is primarily used for quilts with blocks set on point so that the panel, wording, motif, or print are lined up with the direction of the quilt and not turned sideways. Use a 6" x 24" ruler with 45° line; this may require two rulers depending on the length of the fabric.

Accurate Cutting

Make sure you use the same rulers throughout your cutting process; there could be a small variance in the measuring lines of different rulers. To help keep cutting accurate, use thin adhesive tabs or dots of fine-grit sandpaper on the bottom of your rulers so they don't slide while cutting. When you're making multiple cuts, mark the measurement on the ruler with florescent marking tape.

1 Unfold the fabric so it's one layer, 42" wide. Square up the side and bottom of the fabric, cutting off the selvage. Place the 45° line of the ruler at the bottom of the fabric, and then line up the second ruler with the first so that you can make one continuous cut. Cut on the left side of the ruler(s) first.

Align 45° line with bottom edge of fabric.

2 Next, measure the width of the strip required and measure over from the 45° cut line and make the second cut for the strip width. Continue cutting the strips needed by moving the ruler(s) to the right on the 45° angle.

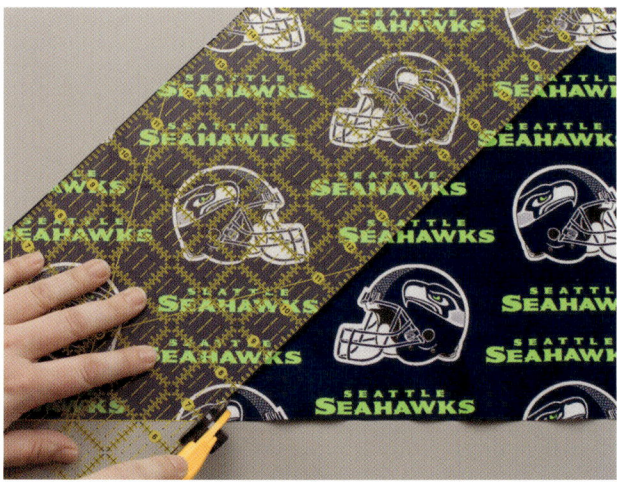

Cut strip the width specified in project instructions.

3 Crosscut the strips in the same way, cutting squares or rectangles from the strips. Handle the pieces carefully, as all the edges will be bias.

SQUARING UP

Once you've sewn the units for the blocks you'll need to square up each sewn piece, especially any half-square-triangle units. Squaring up takes some time, but it's worth it for the accuracy it produces. This technique not only makes the pieces of the block go together easily, but also creates a more precise quilt.

Press all of the units first, and then measure them. Use the smallest measurement to square up all of the units. However, if the measurements vary more than ⅛", check the construction of the units that are affected. You may have to resew some units if there were mistakes in the piecing or cutting. Usually you'll trim off only a tiny amount (threads) if you pieced and cut accurately.

For horizontal and vertical seams, use a square ruler and line up one of the seam lines with one of the lines on the ruler. Trim where needed. For half-square triangles with diagonal seams, use a square ruler and line up the diagonal seam with the diagonal line on the ruler. Slide the ruler if required and keep lining up the diagonal line and seam as needed to trim the square. I suggest moving the ruler and not the unit when squaring up to maintain accuracy.

Align 45° line with the diagonal seam and trim outer edges to size specified in project.

Be aware of intersecting points on the edges of the block. You need a ¼" seam allowance at those intersections so that the points aren't cut off when sewing the blocks together to create the quilt top.

Don't trim off the ¼" seam allowance!

Helpful Tool for Squaring Up Units

A revolving cutting mat is a great tool to use when squaring up units or blocks. Place the piece in the center of the cutting mat and spin the mat around and move the ruler. This way right- and left-handed quilters can trim with ease without moving the fabric itself.

Working with Sports-Theme Prints

Tips for Easy Piecing

The following tips will help you achieve success when piecing. Not only will these ideas work well for the projects in this book, but can also be incorporated into your arsenal of quiltmaking tips for future projects.

Half-square-triangle units. When creating half-square-triangle units, you can sew with a seam allowance that's a few threads narrower than ¼" (often referred to as a "scant ¼" seam allowance") so that the finished square will be the measurement required.

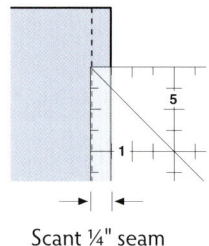

Scant ¼" seam

The other option, which I used in the directions in this book, is to cut the squares ⅛" larger than called for in the instructions, sew the half-square-triangles units, and then square up the completed units to the required measurement, referring to "Squaring Up" on page 9.

Bias edges. Be careful handling fabric cut on the diagonal, since you'll be dealing with bias edges and it's easy to stretch them out of shape. I use spray sizing on fabric *before* cutting on the bias to stabilize the edges.

Measure all blocks. Make sure to measure all the blocks before assembling the quilt top. Use the measurement of the smallest block to square up all the blocks (see "Squaring Up" on page 9). It may be necessary to change the measurements of any sashing pieces or alternate blocks if your blocks are slightly smaller than the size specified in the directions.

Binding

Use a walking foot to stitch the binding to the quilt. This foot works beautifully to prevent the quilt layers from puckering while attaching the binding. Follow these steps for straight-grain binding.

1 To prepare your quilt for binding, baste using a ⅛" seam allowance around the outer edge of the quilt top, and then trim to clean up the edges of the quilt.

2 Measure the top, bottom, and sides of the quilt and total the measurements. Add 12" for joining the ends. Cut 2¼"-wide binding strips totaling the final measurement.

3 Sew the strips together to make one continuous binding strip by placing two strips right sides together, perpendicular to each other as shown. Stitch on the diagonal and trim the seam allowances to ¼". Press the seam allowances open so the binding will lie flat.

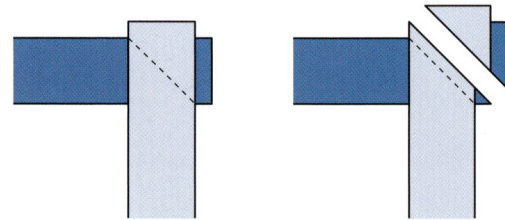

4 Fold the long strip in half lengthwise, wrong sides together, and press.

5 Select a beginning point along one of the lower sides of the quilt top. With right sides together, line up the raw edge of the binding with the raw edge of the quilt top, leaving a 6" tail for joining the ends. Begin stitching using a ¼" seam allowance; backstitch at the beginning. Stop stitching ¼" from the corner, turn the quilt 45°, and stitch to the corner and off the quilt. Remove the quilt from the sewing machine.

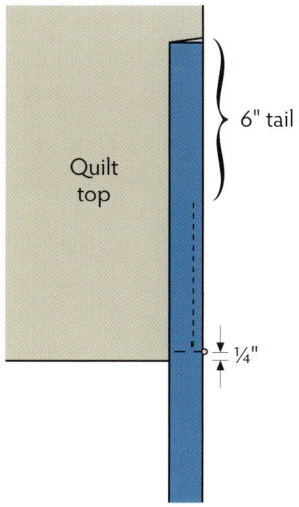

6 Rotate the quilt a quarter turn and fold the binding straight up, forming a 45° fold. Fold the binding strip down and over the fold, with the fold lining up with the previous sewn edge. Align the raw edges of the binding and quilt top and start stitching from the top edge, stitching all the layers. Backstitch, and then continue sewing the binding to this next side of the quilt.

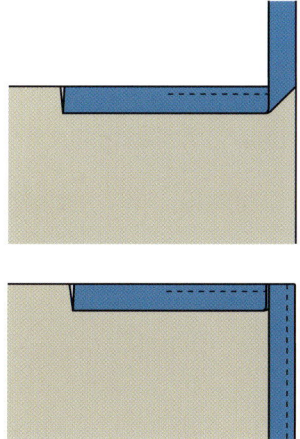

7 Repeat the corner technique on all four corners. Once your stitching gets close to the beginning stitching, end your stitching 12" before the starting place. Backstitch the end stitch and leave the tail for joining the ends.

8 Join by overlapping the binding ends. Measure 2¼" beyond the top binding-end overlap and trim the excess.

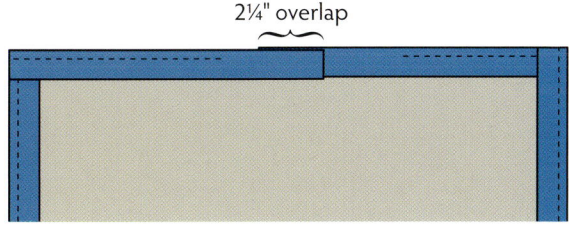

9 Open the folded binding ends and place them right sides together and perpendicular to each other. Sew on the diagonal. Measure ¼" from the stitching line and trim the excess. Press the seam allowances open.

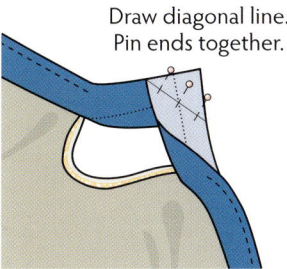 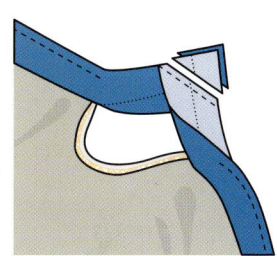

Draw diagonal line. Pin ends together.

10 Refold the binding and line up the raw edges with the quilt top. Finish stitching the binding to the quilt.

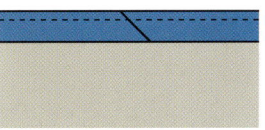

11 Fold the binding over the edge to the back of the quilt and hand stitch the binding to the quilt.

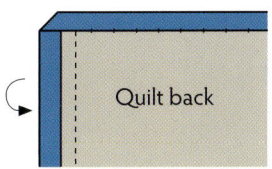 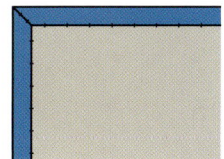

Quilt back

Alternate Colorways

This book contains 11 projects, but sometimes the project design you like uses fabric that just isn't your sport. No worries; simply substitute your favorite team's colors or the sport your love best. Below are examples of alternate color and fabric choices for most of the quilts in this book.

Start Your Engines

Season Tickets

Pregame Warm-Up

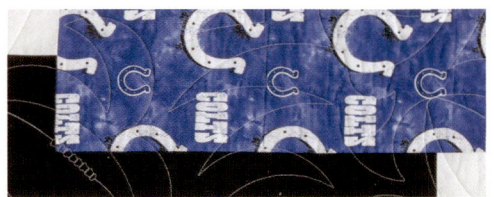

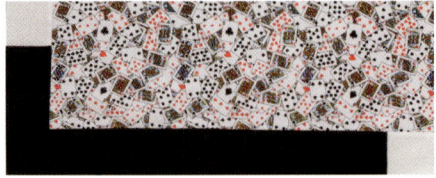

Starting Time

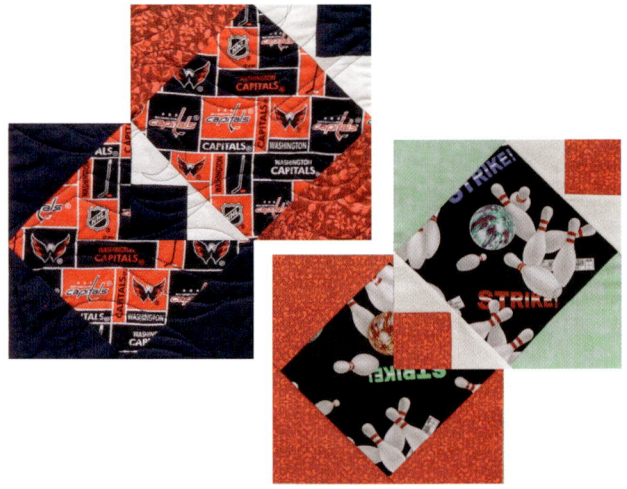

Halftime Event

Friday Night Lights

The Winning Strategy

Go Team!

Going for Overtime

Game Delay

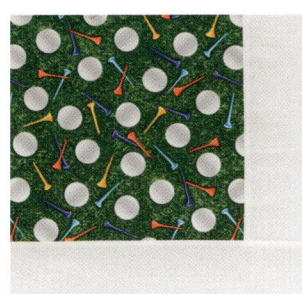

Alternate Colorways 13

START YOUR ENGINES

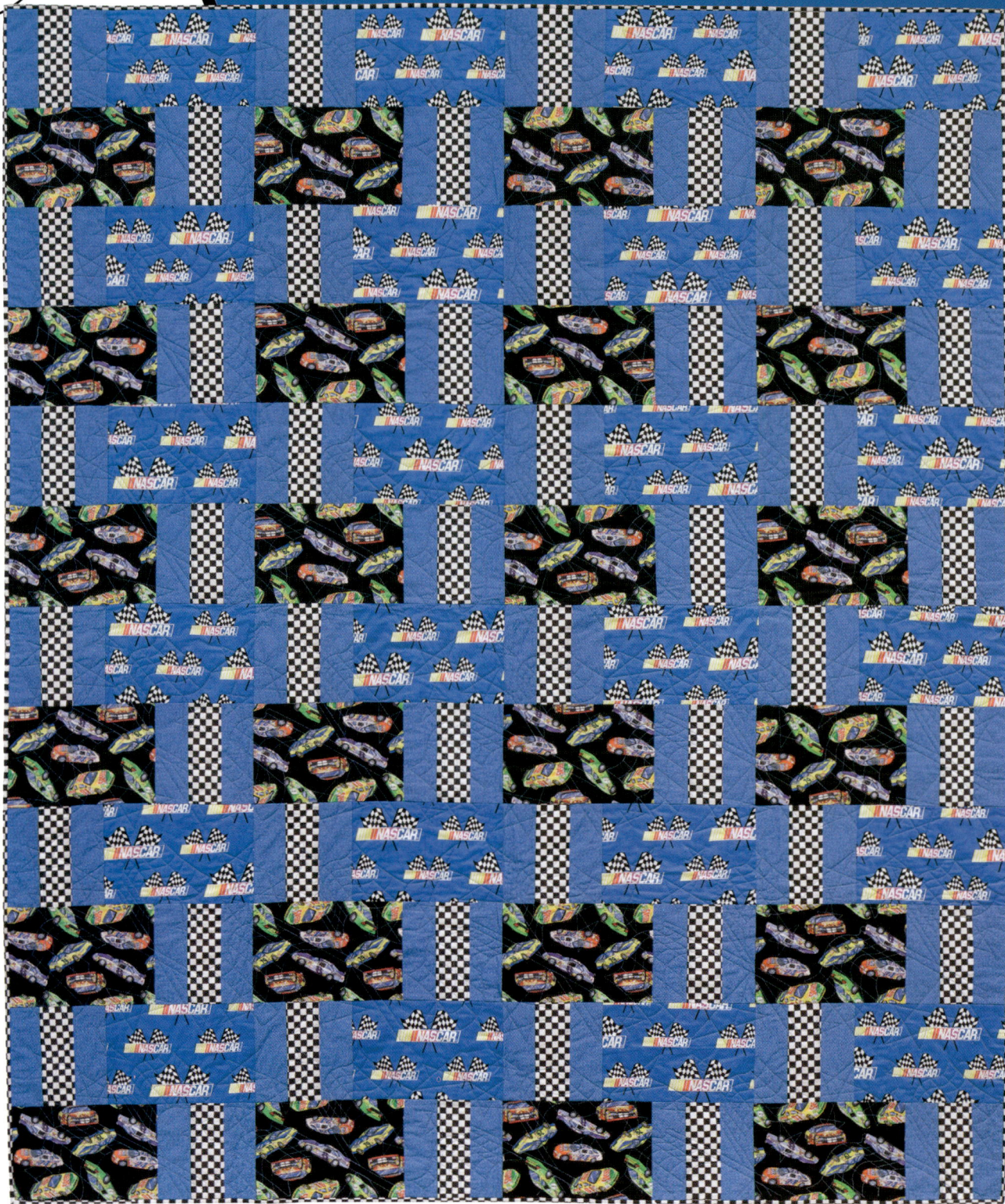

Finished Quilt: 60½" x 72½" | Finished Block: 6" x 6" | Skill level: Beginner

MATERIALS

Yardage is based on 42"-wide fabric unless otherwise noted.

2½ yards of sport-logo print OR 1¼ yard *each* of sport-logo print (race cars) and coordinating novelty print (checkered flags)*

1⅓ yards of blue solid for Rail Fence blocks

1⅛ yards of black-and-white check for Rail Fence blocks and binding

4¾ yards of backing fabric

73" x 85" piece of batting

*If your fabric is 60" wide, you'll need 1⅝ yards of sport-logo print or ⅞ yards each of sport-logo print (race cars) and coordinating novelty print (checkered flags).

CUTTING

From the sport-logo print, cut:

12 strips, 6½" x 42"; crosscut into 48 rectangles, 6½" x 9½"*

From the black-and-white check, cut:

8 strips, 2½" x 42"; crosscut into 48 rectangles, 2½" x 6½"

7 strips, 2¼" x 42"

From the blue solid, cut:

16 strips, 2½" x 42"; crosscut into 96 rectangles, 2½" x 6½"

*If your fabric is 60" wide, you'll only need 8 strips, 6½" x 60". Check your fabric before cutting to make sure the logo fits into the 6½" strip width. If the logo is taller, cut 9½"-wide strips, and then crosscut them into 6½" x 9½" rectangles. If using a combination of logo fabric and coordinating theme print, as in the quilt shown, cut 6 strips of each, and crosscut into 24 rectangles of each fabric.

PIECING THE BLOCKS

Sew a blue 2½" x 6½" rectangle to each side of a check 2½" x 6½" rectangle to make a Rail Fence block. Press the seam allowances toward the blue fabric. Repeat to make a total of 48 blocks.

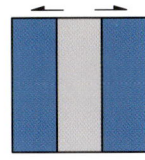

Make 48.

ASSEMBLING THE QUILT TOP

1. Refer to the quit assembly diagram below for making the rows. Lay out the Rail Fence blocks and sport-logo 6½" x 9½" rectangles, alternating them as you go. Start with a Rail Fence in the upper-left corner and end with a print rectangle in the upper-right corner. Make a total of 12 rows with four blocks and four rectangles each. **Note:** If you're using two different prints, use one in the odd-numbered rows and the other in the even-numbered rows.

2. Sew the blocks and rectangles in each row along their 6½" edges and press the seam allowances toward the logo print.

3. Sew the rows together and press the seam allowances all in one direction.

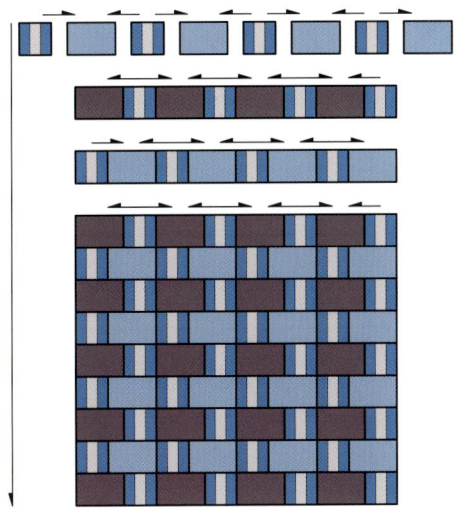

Quilt assembly

FINISHING THE QUILT

For more help on any of the finishing techniques, go to ShopMartingale.com for free downloadable information.

1. Layer the backing, batting, and quilt top; baste.

2. Quilt as desired. In the featured quilt, I stitched an overall design of checkered flags and stars.

3. Bind the quilt using the 2¼"-wide checked strips (see "Binding" on page 10).

SEASON TICKETS

Finished quilt: 85⅜" x 102⅜" | Finished block: 12" x 12" | Skill level: Intermediate

MATERIALS

Yardage is based on 42"-wide fabric unless otherwise noted.

4¾ yards of black solid for Postage Stamp blocks and binding

3½ yards of sport-logo print #1 for large squares*

2⅛ yards of white print for Postage Stamp blocks

1¼ yards of sport-logo print #2 for Postage Stamp blocks**

½ yard of red print for Postage Stamp blocks

8⅛ yards of backing fabric

98" x 115" piece of batting

If your fabric is 60" wide, you'll need 2¼ yards.

**If your fabric is 60" wide, you'll need ⅞ yard.*

CUTTING

From the black solid, cut:

6 strips, 12½" x 42"; crosscut into 90 rectangles, 2½" x 12½"

6 strips, 8½" x 42"; crosscut into 90 rectangles, 2½" x 8½"

10 strips, 2¼" x 42"

From the sport-logo print #1, cut:

15 squares on the diagonal, 12½" x 12½"*

From the white print, cut:

13 strips, 5¼" x 42"; crosscut into 90 squares, 5¼" x 5¼". Cut each square in half diagonally to yield 180 triangles.

From the sport-logo print #2, cut:

6 strips, 6¼" x 42"; crosscut into 36 squares, 6¼" x 6¼"**

From the red print, cut:

2 strips, 6¼" x 42"; crosscut into 9 squares, 6¼" x 6¼"

See "Cutting on the Diagonal" (page 8) for cutting sport-logo prints at a 45°.

**If your fabric is 60" wide, cut 4 strips, 6¼" x 60", and crosscut them into 36 squares, 6¼" x 6¼".*

PIECING THE BLOCKS

1 Sew white 5¼" triangles to opposite sides of a 6¼" sport-logo #2 square. Press the seam allowances toward the triangles. Sew a white triangle to the top and bottom of the squares. Press the seam allowances toward the triangles. Square the block to 8½" x 8½". **Note:** Use a true ¼" seam allowance, not a scant one.

Make 36.

2 Sew black 2½" x 8½" rectangles to the top and bottom of the block and press the seam allowances toward the black fabric. Sew black 2½" x 12½" rectangles to the sides of the block and press. The block should measure 12½" x 12½". Repeat to make a total of 36 blocks.

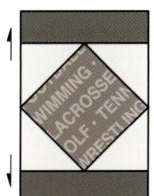 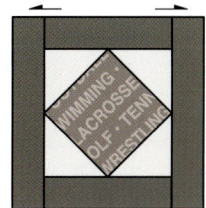

Make 36.

Help for Bias Edges

You'll be sewing the bias edges of the triangles to the 6¼" squares. Using spray sizing on the fabric *before* cutting will help stabilize the edges and reduce stretching while sewing. Press the seam allowances toward the darker fabric. You'll end up with a block that looks crisp and finished.

3 Follow steps 1 and 2 to make nine blocks using red 6¼" squares in the center. Cut each square in half diagonally to make 18 side triangles.

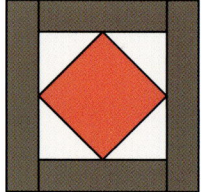
Make 9.

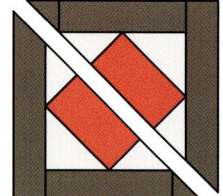
Make 18.

4 Cut two of the 12½" squares in half diagonally. Be careful when cutting directional fabric; check to make sure that the logo is going in the correct direction before cutting the square. The logo can go up and down or sideways, depending on the way you cut your square. Cut in half so that the logo runs along the long side of the triangle. To keep the edges tame, spray starch on the square before cutting.

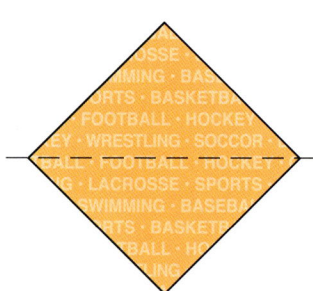
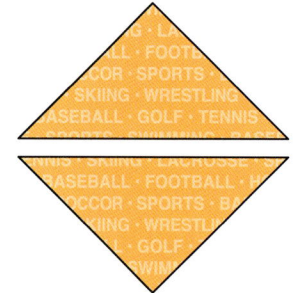

ASSEMBLING THE QUILT TOP

1 Lay out the blocks, half-blocks, and sport-logo print #1 squares into 11 diagonal rows, following the quilt assembly diagram at right. Sew the units together into rows and press the seam allowances in opposite directions from row to row.

2 Sew the rows together and press the seam allowances in one direction.

Quilt assembly

FINISHING THE QUILT

For more help on any of the finishing techniques, go to ShopMartingale.com for free downloadable information.

1 Layer the backing, batting, and quilt top; baste.

2 Quilt as desired. I quilted footballs and loops throughout.

3 Bind the quilt using the black 2¼"-wide strips (see "Binding" on page 10).

Folded-Corner Method

If you prefer to sew this quilt using the folded-corner method, you'll need to purchase the following amounts of fabric. All other fabric requirements remain the same.

2⅓ yards of sport-logo print #2

⅞ yard of red print

3¼ yards of white print

Cut 36 diagonal-cut squares, 8½" x 8½", from the sport-logo print #2. (See "Cutting on the Diagonal" on page 8 for cutting sport-logo prints at a 45° angle.) Cut 9 squares, 8½" x 8½", from the red print. Finally, cut 180 squares, 4½" x 4½", from the white print.

1 On the wrong side of the white 4½" squares, draw a diagonal line from corner to corner.

2 Place a marked square, right sides together, on the corner of an 8½" sport-logo #2 square. Sew directly on the line, pressing the seam allowances away from the sport print, and trim the bottom two layers, leaving a ¼" seam allowance. Repeat for the remaining corners. Repeat to make a total of 36.

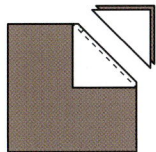 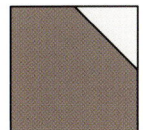 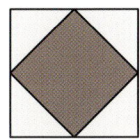

Make 36.

3 Repeat with the red 8½" squares. Make nine.

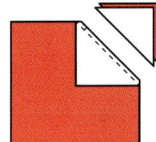 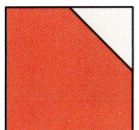 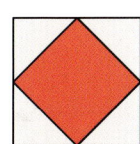

Make 9.

 ## Not Your Sport? Try This...

PREGAME WARM-UP

Finished quilt: 56½" x 74½" | Finished block: 8" x 20" | Skill level: Easy

MATERIALS

Yardage is based on 42"-wide fabric.

2⅛ yards of white print for blocks, sashing, and border

1⅓ yards of black solid for blocks and binding

⅝ yard *each* of 13 different sport-logo prints*

⅓ yard of football print for offset rectangles

4⅞ yards of backing fabric

69" x 87" piece of batting

*Check your fabric before purchasing to make sure the logos are printed lengthwise, running parallel to the selvage. If the logos are printed perpendicular to the selvage, you'll only need ⅓ yard of each instead.

CUTTING

From the white print, cut:

4 strips, 2½" x 42"; crosscut into 8 rectangles, 2½" x 8½", and 26 squares, 2½" x 2½"

7 strips, 2½" x 42"

2 strips, 3½" x 42"; crosscut into 6 rectangles, 3½" x 8½"

8 strips, 4½" x 42"

From the black solid, cut:

1 strip, 16½" x 42"; crosscut into 13 rectangles, 2½" x 16½"

1 strip, 6½" x 42"; crosscut into 13 rectangles, 2½" x 6½"

7 strips, 2¼" x 42"

From *each* sport-logo print, cut:

1 rectangle, 6½" x 18½" (13 total)*

From the football print, cut:

1 strip, 8½" x 42"; crosscut into 6 rectangles, 6½" x 8½"

*When cutting the 6½" x 18½" rectangles, make sure the logos will be right side up (they should run lengthwise).

PIECING THE BLOCKS AND SASHING UNITS

1 Sew a white 2½" square to one end of each black 2½" x 16½" rectangle. In the same manner, sew a white 2½" square to the end of a black 2½" x 6½" rectangle. Press the seam allowances toward the black rectangles. Make 13 of each.

Make 13 of each.

2 Sew the long unit from step 1 to the right side of a sport-logo rectangle, making sure that the white square is at the top. Press the seam allowances toward the logo print. Sew the short unit from step 1 to the bottom of the piece, making sure that the white square is on the bottom left. Press the seam allowances toward the logo fabric. The block should measure 8½" x 20½". Repeat for all 13 sport-logo rectangles.

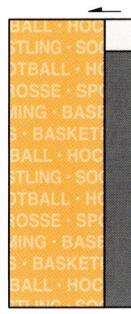 

Make 13.

Using the Leftovers

You'll have quite a bit of assorted logo-print fabrics left over from making this quilt. Here are some ideas for putting them to good use:

- Make coordinating pillowcases or pillow shams.
- Incorporate them into the quilt backing.
- Use them to make "Game Delay" on page 37.

3 Sew white 3½" x 8½" rectangles to the top and bottom of *three* blocks from step 2. Press the seam allowances toward the white fabric.

Make 3.

4 To make the offset rectangle units, sew a white 2½" x 8½" rectangle to a football-print 6½" x 8½" rectangle. Press the seam allowances toward the football fabric. Repeat to make four. Sew white 2½" x 8½" rectangles to the top and bottom of a football 6½" x 8½" rectangle. Press the seam allowances toward the football fabric. Repeat to make two. **Note:** If your fabric is directional, pay attention to the position of the white rectangle. You may need to sew two to the top of the football fabric and two to the bottom as shown.

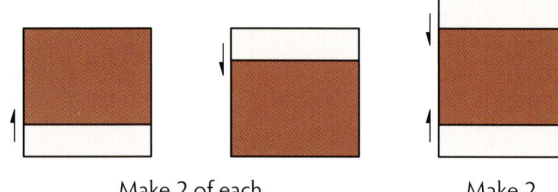

Make 2 of each.   Make 2.

ASSEMBLING THE QUILT TOP

1 Referring to the quilt assembly diagram at right, lay out five vertical rows of blocks and offset rectangle units. Sew the units in each row together from top to bottom, and then press the seam allowances in one direction. The rows should measure 66½" long. Sew the seven white 2½"-wide strips together, end to end. From this strip, cut four strips, 2½" x 66½", for the sashing rows. Sew the sashing rows and block rows together as shown. Press the seam allowances toward the sashing strips.

2 Stitch the eight white 4½"-wide strips together, end to end. Measure the quilt through the center from top and bottom and trim two strips to that measurement. Sew the strips to the sides of the quilt top. Press the seam allowances toward the border strips.

3 Measure the quilt through the center from side to side, including the borders just added. Cut two strips to fit that measurement. Sew the strips to the top and bottom edges of the quilt top; press.

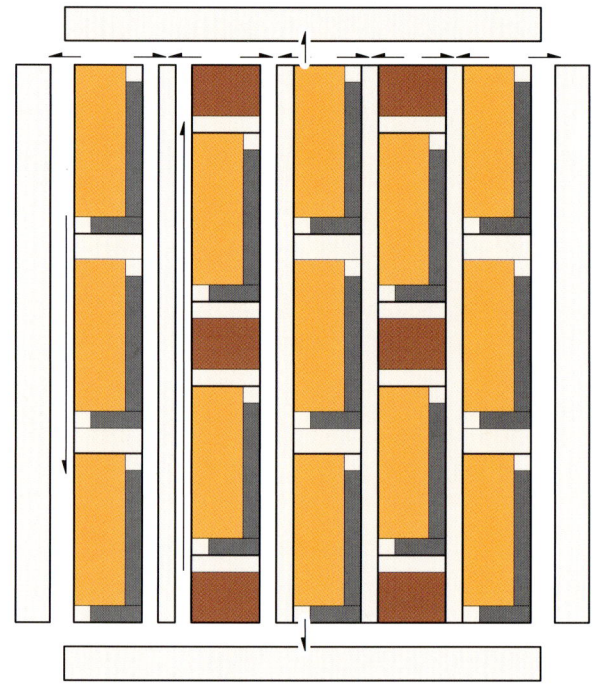

Quilt assembly

FINISHING THE QUILT

For more help on any of the finishing techniques, go to ShopMartingale.com for free downloadable information.

1 Layer the backing, batting, and quilt top; baste.

2 Quilt as desired. I quilted an allover design of footballs and zigzags.

3 Bind the quilt using the black 2¼"-wide strips (see "Binding" on page 10).

STARTING TIME

Finished quilt: 55½" x 72½" | Finished block: 8½" x 8½" | Skill level: Intermediate

MATERIALS

Yardage is based on 42"-wide fabric unless otherwise noted.

2 yards of navy solid for blocks, border, and binding

1¼ yards of sport-logo print for blocks*

1¼ yards of red tone on tone for blocks

1⅛ yards of white tone on tone for blocks

4¾ yards of backing fabric

68" x 85" piece of batting

*If your fabric is 60" wide, you'll need 1 yard.

CUTTING

From the navy solid, cut:

- 3 strips, 5" x 42"; crosscut into 24 squares, 5" x 5". Cut each square in half diagonally to yield 48 triangles.
- 2 strips, 5½" x 42"; crosscut into 12 squares, 5½" x 5½". Cut each square in half diagonally to yield 24 triangles.
- 2 strips, 2½" x 42"; crosscut into 24 squares, 2½" x 2½"
- 7 strips, 2½" x 42"
- 7 strips, 2¼" x 42"

From the sport-logo print, cut:

- 24 diagonal-cut squares, 6½" x 6½"*

From the red tone on tone, cut:

- 3 strips, 9½" x 42"; crosscut into 12 squares, 9½" x 9½"
- 2 strips, 5" x 42"; crosscut into 12 squares, 5" x 5". Cut each square in half diagonally to yield 24 triangles.

From the white tone on tone, cut:

- 3 strips, 9½" x 42"; crosscut into 12 squares, 9½" x 9½"
- 2 strips, 3" x 42"; crosscut into 24 squares, 3" x 3". Cut each square in half diagonally to yield 48 triangles.

*See "Cutting on the Diagonal" (page 8) for cutting sport-logo prints at a 45°.

PIECING BLOCK A

Sew navy 5" triangles to opposite sides of a sport-logo 6½" square. Press the seam allowances toward the navy triangles. Sew two more navy 5" triangles to the remaining sides of the square; press. The block should measure 9" x 9". Repeat to make 12 of block A.

Block A.
Make 12.

PIECING BLOCK B

1 On the wrong sides of the white 9½" squares, draw a diagonal line from corner to corner. Place a marked white square on a red 9½" square, right sides together. Sew ¼" from both sides of the marked line, and then cut directly on the line. Press the seam allowances toward the red triangles. Square the blocks to 9" x 9". Repeat to make a total of 24.

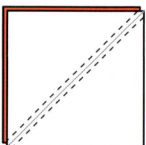 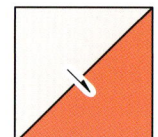 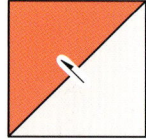

Make 24.

2 Measure 3¼" from the center seam on the red triangle and trim off the block corner as shown. Repeat for all 24 squares.

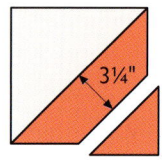

Make 24.

3 Sew a navy 5½" triangle to the cut edge. Press the seam allowances toward the navy triangle. The block should measure 9" x 9". Repeat to make 24 of block B.

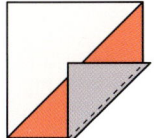 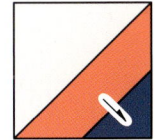

Block B.
Make 24.

PIECING BLOCK C

1 Sew a white 3" triangle to the top of a navy 2½" square. Press the seam allowances toward the navy square. Sew another white 3" triangle to the adjacent side. Press the seam allowances toward the white. Repeat to make a total of 24 units. The 3" triangles are a bit oversized. If needed, trim the point to a ¼" seam allowance.

 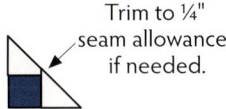

Trim to ¼" seam allowance, if needed.

Make 24.

2 Sew units from step 1 to opposite sides of a sport-logo 6½" square. Press the seam allowances toward the sport-logo print. Sew red 5" triangles to the remaining sides of the unit. Press the seam allowances toward the red triangles. Repeat to make 24 of block C.

Block C.
Make 12.

ASSEMBLING THE QUILT TOP

1 Lay out the A, B, and C blocks referring to the quilt assembly diagram above right. Sew the blocks together in rows and press the seam allowances in opposite directions from row to row.

Join the rows and press all seam allowances in one direction.

2 Sew the navy 2½"-wide strips together, end to end. Measure the quilt through the center from top and bottom and cut two navy strips to that length. Sew the strips to the sides of the quilt top. Press the seam allowances toward the border strips.

3 Measure the quilt through the center from side to side, including the borders just added. Cut two strips to that measurement. Sew the strips to the top and bottom edges of the quilt top; press.

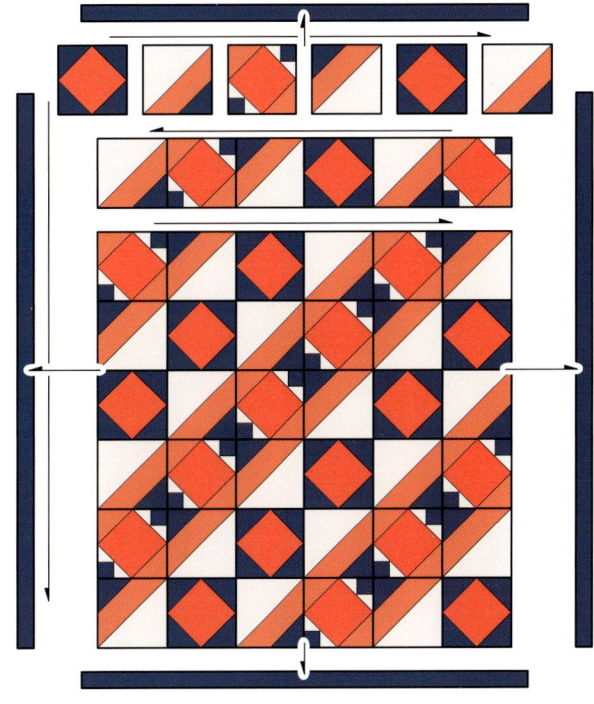

Quilt assembly

FINISHING THE QUILT

For more help on any of the finishing techniques, go to ShopMartingale.com for free downloadable information.

1 Layer the backing, batting, and quilt top; baste.

2 Quilt as desired. I quilted the entire top with swirls and crossed hockey sticks.

3 Bind the quilt using the navy 2¼"-wide strips (see "Binding" on page 10).

HALFTIME EVENT

Finished quilt: 90½" x 101½" | Finished block: 12" x 12" | Skill level: Intermediate

MATERIALS

Yardage is based on 42"-wide fabric unless otherwise noted.

3¼ yards of dark-purple print #1 for Boxed In blocks, border, and binding

1⅝ yards of dark-purple print #2 for Attic Windows blocks

1¾ yards of medium-gold print for Boxed In blocks

1⅜ yards of dark-gold print for Attic Windows blocks

1⅞ yards of sport-logo print #1 for Attic Windows blocks*

1⅜ yards of sport-logo print #2 for Boxed In blocks**

8⅝ yards of backing fabric

103" x 115" piece of batting

Optional: The Angler 2 for diagonal sewing

If your fabric is 60" wide, you'll need 1⅓ yards.

If your fabric is 60" wide, you'll need 1 yard.

CUTTING

From the dark-purple print #1, cut:

19 strips, 3" x 42"; crosscut into:
  28 rectangles, 3" x 12½"
  28 rectangles, 3" x 7½"
  28 squares, 3" x 3"
10 strips, 3½" x 42"
10 strips, 2¼" x 42"

From the dark-purple print #2, cut:

4 strips, 8½" x 42"; crosscut into 28 rectangles, 8½" x 4½"
4 strips, 4½" x 42"; crosscut into 28 squares, 4½" x 4½"

From the medium-gold print, cut:

19 strips, 3" x 42"; crosscut into:
  28 rectangles, 3" x 12½"
  28 rectangles, 3" x 7½"
  28 squares, 3" x 3"

From the dark-gold print, cut:

10 strips, 4½" x 42"; crosscut into 28 rectangles, 4½" x 12½"

From the sport-logo print #1, cut:

7 strips, 8½" x 42"; crosscut into 28 squares, 8½" x 8½"*

From the sport-logo print #2, cut:

6 strips, 7½" x 42"; crosscut into 28 squares, 7½" x 7½"**

If your fabric is 60" wide, cut 5 strips, 8½" x 60", and crosscut them into 28 squares, 8½" x 8½".

If your fabric is 60" wide, cut 4 strips, 7½" x 60", and crosscut them into 28 squares, 7½" x 7½".

PIECING THE ATTIC WINDOWS BLOCKS

1 On the wrong sides of the dark-purple 4½" squares, draw a diagonal line from corner to corner.

2 With right sides together, place a marked 4½" square on a dark-gold 4½" x 12½" rectangle. Sew directly on the line, making sure the diagonal direction matches the diagram. Trim the excess seam allowances to ¼", and then press the seam allowances toward the purple. Repeat to make 28.

Make 28.

3 Sew a dark-purple 4½" x 8½" rectangle to the left side of an 8½" square of sport-logo #1. Press the seam allowance toward the logo print. Repeat to make 28.

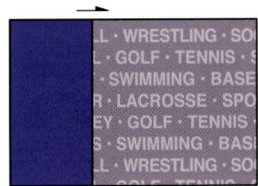

Make 28.

4 Sew a unit from step 2 unit to the bottom of a unit from step 3. Press the seam allowances toward the top unit. Repeat to make 28. The block should measure 12½" x 12½".

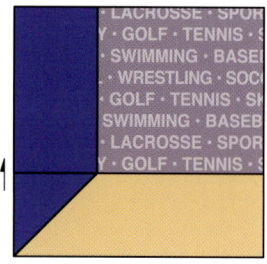

Make 28.

PIECING THE BOXED IN BLOCKS

1 On the wrong sides of the dark-purple and medium-gold 3" squares, draw a diagonal line from corner to corner.

 Easy Diagonals

Instead of drawing a diagonal line on the wrong side of each square, save yourself some time with a specialty tool. The Angler 2 is a sheet of clear plastic that you tape in place our your sewing-machine bed. It has marked guidelines to make sewing on the diagonal easy and accurate—without having to mark your fabrics.

2 With right sides together, place a marked dark-purple 3" square on a medium-gold 3" x 12½" rectangle, making sure the diagonal direction matches the diagram. Sew directly on the line to make a top section. Trim the excess seam allowances to ¼", and then press toward the purple. Make 28.

Make 28.

3 With right sides together, place a marked medium-gold 3" square on a dark-purple 3" x 12½" rectangle, making sure the diagonal direction matches the diagram. Sew directly on the line to make a bottom section. Trim the excess seam allowances to ¼", and then press toward the gold. Make 28.

Make 28.

4 Sew a medium-gold 3" x 7½" rectangle to the right side of a 7½" sport-logo #2 square. Sew a dark-purple 3" x 7½" rectangle to the left side to make a center section. Press away from the logo print. Repeat to make 28.

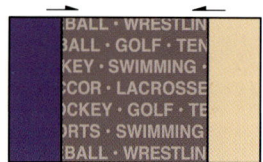

Make 28.

5 Sew together the top, center, and bottom units, taking care to match the placement of fabrics as shown. Repeat to make a total of 28 blocks. The blocks should measure 12½" x 12½".

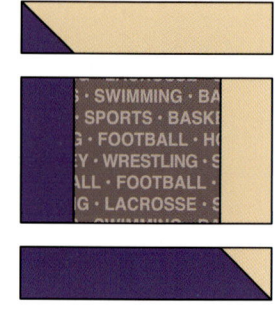 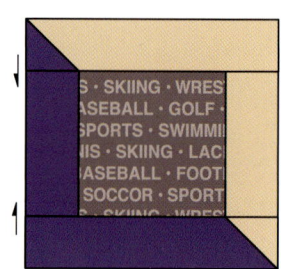

Make 28.

ASSEMBLING THE QUILT TOP

1 Lay out the blocks into rows as shown in the quilt assembly diagram at right, alternating the Attic Window blocks and the Boxed In blocks. Sew the blocks into rows. Press the seam allowances in opposite directions from row to row. Sew the rows together and press all the seam allowances in one direction.

Matching Diagonal Intersecting Points

To match the diagonal seams when constructing the block, place a pin in the diagonal seam, ¼" in from the seam allowance. Now place that same pin in the seam, ¼" in from the seam allowance, and pin the two pieces together with the pin in place so that the seams will meet once sewn. Also place a pin on either side of the intersecting seam to stop the fabric from sliding. Fork pins could be used for this. When you begin stitching, leave the pin in place until your sewing machine needle is one stitch away from it. Remove the pins as you reach them; do not sew over them.

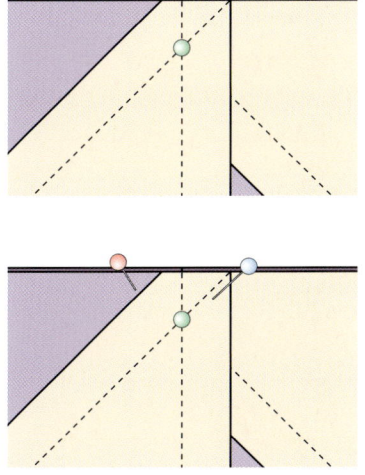

2 Sew the dark-purple 3½"-wide strips together, end to end. Measure the quilt through the center from top to bottom and cut two dark-purple strips to that measurement. Sew the strips to the sides of the quilt top. Press the seam allowances toward the border strips.

3 Measure the quilt through the center from side to side, including the borders just added. Cut two strips to that measurement. Sew the strips to the top and bottom edges of the quilt top; press.

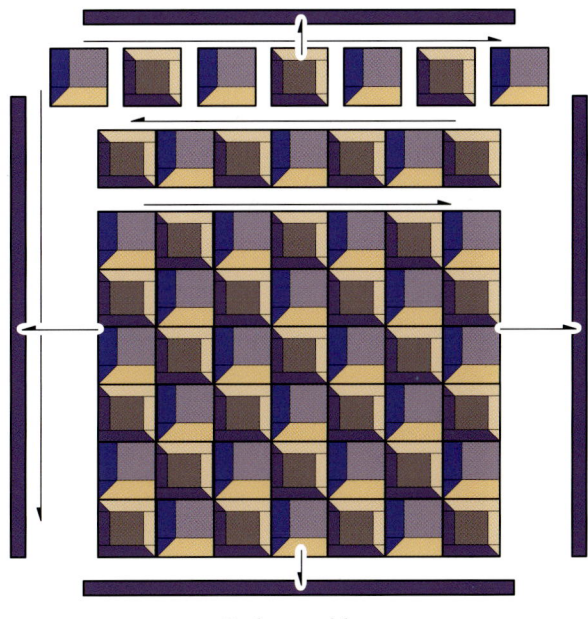

Quilt assembly

FINISHING THE QUILT

For more help on any of the finishing techniques, go to ShopMartingale.com for free downloadable information.

1 Layer the backing, batting, and quilt top; baste.

2 Quilt as desired. I quilted an allover design of swirls and curls.

3 Bind the quilt using the dark-purple 2¼"-wide strips (see "Binding" on page 10).

FRIDAY NIGHT LIGHTS

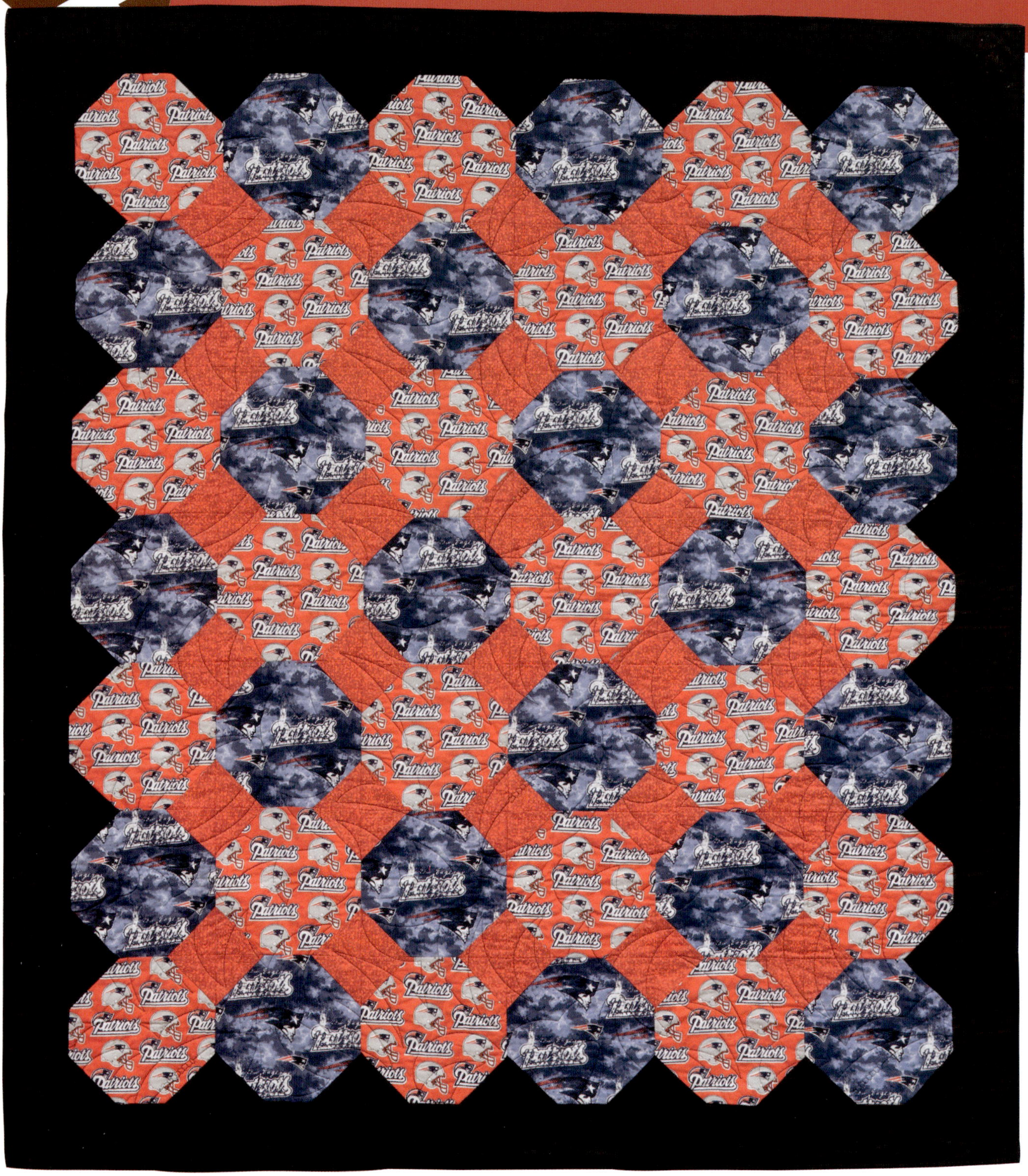

Finished quilt: 63½" x 72" | Finished block: 9" x 9" | Skill level: Easy

MATERIALS

Yardage is based on 42"-wide fabric unless otherwise noted.

2 yards of black solid for blocks, border, and binding

1¾ yards of sport-logo print #1 for blocks*

1¾ yards of sport-logo print #2 for blocks*

1¼ yards of red print for blocks

4¼ yards of backing fabric

75" x 80" piece of batting

Optional: The Angler 2 for sewing diagonal seams

*If your fabric is 60" wide, you'll need 1¼ yards.

CUTTING

From the black solid, cut:

    5 strips, 3½" x 42"; crosscut into 48 squares, 3½" x 3½"

    7 strips, 4½" x 42"

    7 strips, 2¼" x 42"

From the sport-logo print #1, cut:

    6 strips, 9½" x 42"; crosscut into 21 squares, 9½" x 9½"*

From the sport-logo print #2, cut:

    6 strips, 9½" x 42"; crosscut into 21 squares, 9½" x 9½"*

From the red print, cut:

    11 strips, 3½" x 42"; crosscut into 120 squares, 3½" x 3½"

*If your fabric is 60" wide, cut 4 strips, 9½" x 60", and crosscut them into 21 squares, 9½" x 9½".

PIECING THE BLOCKS

1 On the backs of the red and black 3½" squares, draw a diagonal line from corner to corner.

2 Place a marked red 3½" square on each corner of a 9½" sport-logo #1 square. Sew directly on the lines to form the Snowball block. Trim the excess seam allowances to ¼". Press the seam allowances on the top-right and bottom-left corners toward the triangles and those on the top-left and bottom-right corners toward the center square. Repeat to make 10 blocks using sport-logo #1 (block A) and 10 using sport-logo #2 (block B).

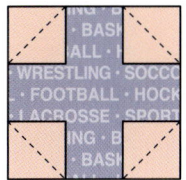 

Block A.
Make 10.

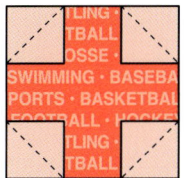 

Block B.
Make 10.

3 Referring to step 2, use the red and black 3½" squares on the 9½" sport-logo squares to make the following blocks in the quantities specified. Be sure to orient your logo fabric so it's always upright as you sew on the corners so that the blocks in your finished quilt top will all be oriented the same way. Press the seam allowances as indicated by the pressing arrows in each illustration.

Block C. **Block D.**

Make 2 of each.

Block E. **Block F.**

Make 2 of each.

Block G. **Block H.**
Make 2. Make 3.

Block I. **Block J.**
Make 3. Make 2.

Block K. **Block L.**
Make 1 for right upper corner. Make 1 for left upper corner.

Block M. **Block N.**
Make 1 for right lower corner. Make 1 for left lower corner.

ASSEMBLING THE QUILT TOP

1 Lay out the blocks in rows according to the quilt assembly diagram on page 33. Be careful to orient the blocks correctly. Sew the blocks into rows and press the seam allowances in opposite directions from row to row. Join the rows and press the seam allowances in one direction.

2 Sew the black 4½"-wide strips together, end to end. Measure the quilt through the center from top and bottom and cut two 4½"-wide strips to that length. Sew the strips to the sides of the quilt top. Press the seam allowances toward the border strips.

3 Measure the quilt through the center from side to side, including the borders just added. Cut two strips to that measurement. Sew the strips to the top and bottom edges of the quilt top; press.

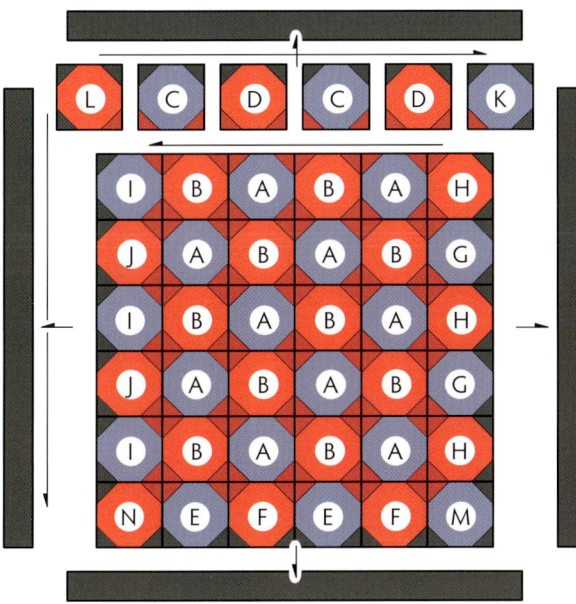

Quilt assembly

FINISHING THE QUILT

For more help on any of the finishing techniques, go to ShopMartingale.com for free downloadable information.

1 Layer the backing, batting, and quilt top; baste.

2 Quilt as desired. I quilted footballs and loops throughout.

3 Bind the quilt using the black 2¼"-wide strips (see "Binding" on page 10).

Not Your Sport? Try This...

Friday Night Lights **33**

GO TEAM!

Finished quilt: 80½" x 92½"　　**Finished block:** 12" x 12"　　**Skill level:** Intermediate

MATERIALS

Yardage is based on 42"-wide fabric unless otherwise noted.

4 yards of sport-logo print for blocks and border*

3¼ yards of white print for blocks

2⅓ yards of gray print for blocks and binding

7¾ yards of backing fabric

93" x 105" piece of batting

Optional: The Angler 2 for sewing diagonal seams and your favorite specialty ruler for making half-square triangles

*If your fabric is 60" wide, you'll need 3⅓ yards.

CUTTING

From the sport-logo print, cut from the *crosswise* grain*:

2 strips, 4½" x 42"; crosscut into 14 squares, 4½" x 4½"**

5 strips, 4½" x 42"; set aside for top and bottom borders

From the remainder of the sport-logo print, cut from the *lengthwise* grain*:

2 strips, 4½" x 90"; set aside for side borders

From the remainder of the sport-logo print, cut from the *crosswise* grain*:

14 strips, 5" x 33"; crosscut into 84 squares, 5" x 5"

4 strips, 4½" x 33"; crosscut into 28 squares, 4½" x 4½"**

From the white print, cut:

21 strips, 5" x 42"; crosscut into 168 squares, 5" x 5"

From the gray print, cut:

11 strips, 5" x 42"; crosscut into 84 squares, 5" x 5"

9 strips, 2¼" x 42"

*If your fabric is 60" wide, instead cut:

From the sport-logo print, cut from the lengthwise grain:
2 strips, 4½" x 90"

From the remaining sport-logo print, cut from the crosswise grain:
10 strips, 5" x 51"; crosscut into 84 squares, 5" x 5"
5 strips, 4½" x 51"; crosscut into 42 squares, 4½" x 4½"**
4 strips, 4½" x 51"

**These squares are for the block centers. If you're going to fussy cut them, you may need additional fabric to cut additional strips.

PIECING THE BLOCKS

1 On the wrong side of each white 5" square, draw a diagonal line from corner to corner.

2 Place a marked white square on a gray 5" square, right sides together. Sew ¼" from both sides of the drawn line. Make 84. Cut on the drawn line, yielding two half-square triangles, and press the seam allowances toward the gray. Square the units to 4½" x 4½". Repeat to make a total of 168.

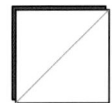 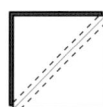 

Make 168.

Half-Square-Triangle Logo Direction

To have the sport-logo points facing the same direction, refer to the diagram below to make the top and bottom units with one half-square triangle and the left and right units with a second half-square triangle.

Make 42.   Yields 84.

 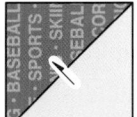 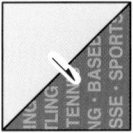

Make 42.   Yields 84.

Go Team! 35

3 Repeat step 2 using white and sport-logo 5" squares. Make a total of 168.

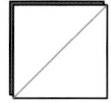 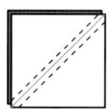 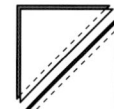

Make 168.

4 Lay out four units from step 2, four units from step 3, and one sport-logo 4½" square as shown. Sew the block together, pressing the seam allowances as indicated by the arrows. The block should measure 12½" x 12½". Repeat to make a total of 42 blocks.

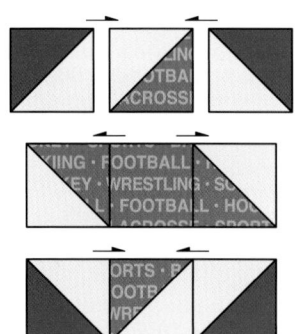 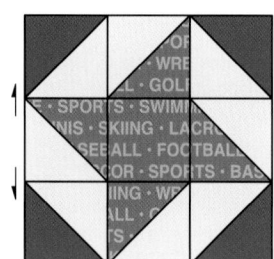

Make 42.

ASSEMBLING THE QUILT TOP

1 Lay out the blocks, following the quilt assembly diagram above right. Sew the blocks into rows. Press the seam allowances in opposite directions from row to row. Join the rows and press all the seam allowances in one direction.

2 Measure the quilt through the center from top and bottom and cut two sport-logo strips to that measurement. Note the direction of the sports logo. Sew the strips to the sides of the quilt top. Press the seam allowances toward the border strips.

3 Measure the quilt through the center from side to side, including the borders just added. Cut two strips to fit that measurement, being careful of the direction of the sports logo. Sew the strips to the top and bottom of the quilt top; press.

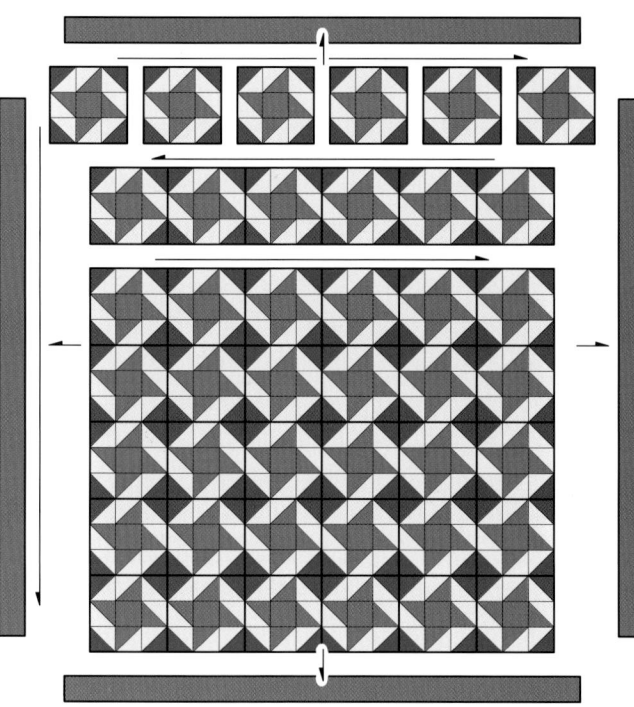

Quilt assembly

FINISHING THE QUILT

For more help on any of the finishing techniques, go to ShopMartingale.com for free downloadable information.

1 Layer the backing, batting, and quilt top; baste.

2 Quilt as desired. I quilted an overall design of footballs and loops.

3 Bind the quilt using the gray 2¼"-wide strips (see "Binding" on page 10).

GAME DELAY

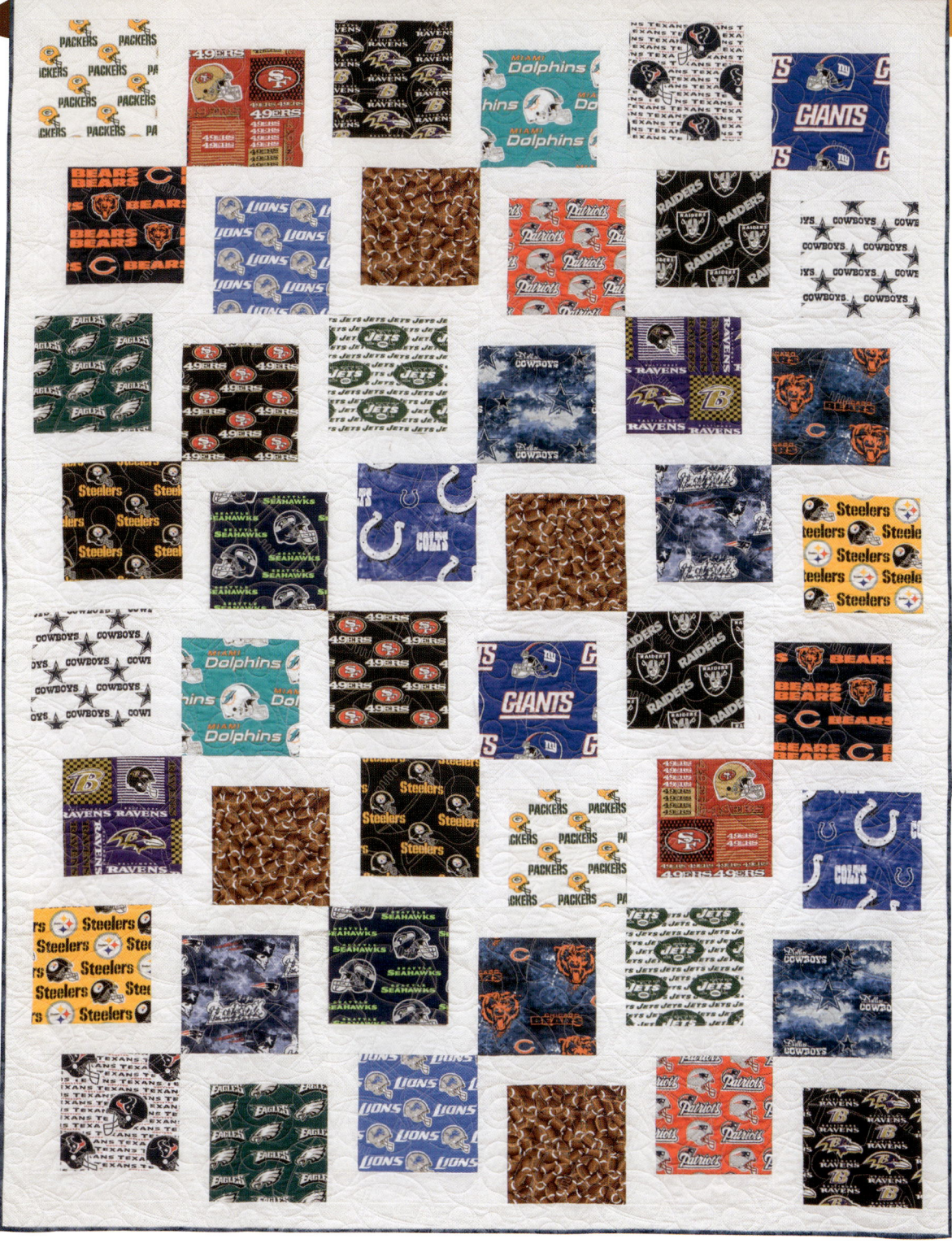

Finished quilt: 64½" x 84½" | Finished block: 10" x 10" | Skill Level: Easy

37

MATERIALS

Yardage is based on 42"-wide fabric.

⅓ yard *each* of 22 different sport-logo prints for blocks

2⅜ yards of white print for blocks and border

⅓ yard of football print for blocks

⅝ yards of blue print for binding

5⅜ yards of backing fabric

77" x 97" piece of batting

CUTTING

From the white print, cut:

 3 strips, 10½" x 42"; crosscut into 48 rectangles, 2½" x 10½"

 3 strips, 8½" x 42"; crosscut into 48 rectangles, 2½" x 8½"

 8 strips, 2½" x 42"

From *each* of the sport-logo prints, cut:

 1 strip, 8½" x 42"; crosscut into 2 squares, 8½" x 8½" (44 total)

From the football print, cut:

 1 strip, 8½" x 42"; crosscut into 4 squares, 8½" x 8½"

From the blue print, cut:

 8 strips, 2¼" x 42"

PIECING BLOCK A

Choose 12 different sport-logo 8½" squares. Sew a white 2½" x 8½" rectangle to the right edge of each square. Press the seam allowances toward the squares. Sew a white 2½" x 10½" rectangle to the bottom of each unit. Press the seam allowances toward the squares. The blocks should measure 10½" square.

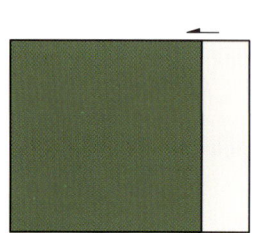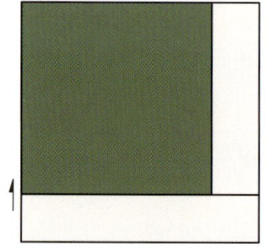

Block A.
Make 12.

PIECING BLOCK B

Choose 12 different sport-logo 8½" squares. Sew a white 2½" x 8½" rectangle to the right edge of each square. Press the seam allowances toward the squares. Sew a white 2½" x 10½" rectangle to the top of each unit. Press the seam allowances toward the squares. The blocks should measure 10½" square.

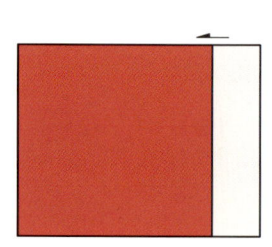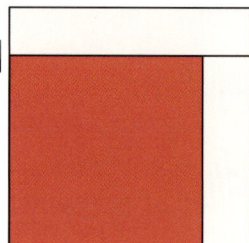

Block B.
Make 12.

PIECING BLOCK C

Choose 11 different sport-logo 8½" squares and one football 8½" square. Sew a white 2½" x 8½" rectangle to the left side of each square. Press the seam allowances toward the squares. Sew a white 2½" x 10½" rectangle to the bottom of each unit. Press the seam allowances toward the squares. The blocks should measure 10½" square.

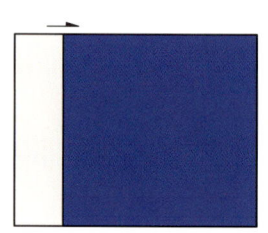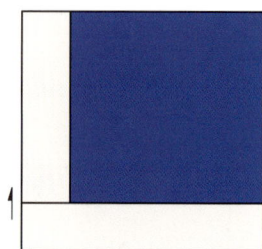

Block C.
Make 11 sports-logo and 1 football.

PIECING BLOCK D

Choose nine different sport-logo 8½" squares and three football 8½" squares. Sew a white 2½" x 8½" rectangle to the left side of each square. Press the seam allowances toward the squares. Sew a white 2½" x 10½" rectangle to the top of the units. Press the seam allowances toward the squares. The blocks should measure 10½" square.

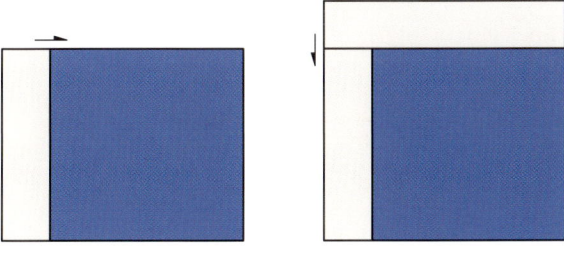

Block D.
Make 9 sports-logo and 3 football.

ASSEMBLING THE QUILT TOP

1. Lay out the blocks according to quilt assembly diagram above right. Rows 1, 3, 5, and 7, alternate blocks A and B, starting with block A. Rows 2, 4, 6, and 8, alternate blocks C and D, starting with block C. Sew the blocks into rows. Press the seam allowances in opposite directions from row to row. Join the rows and press the seam allowances in one direction.

2. Sew the white 2½"-wide strips together, end to end. Measure the quilt through the center from top and bottom and cut two white strips to that measurement. Sew the strips to the sides of the quilt top. Press the seam allowances toward the border strips.

3. Measure the quilt through the center from side to side, including the borders just added. Cut two strips to that measurement. Sew the strips to the top and bottom edges of the quilt top; press.

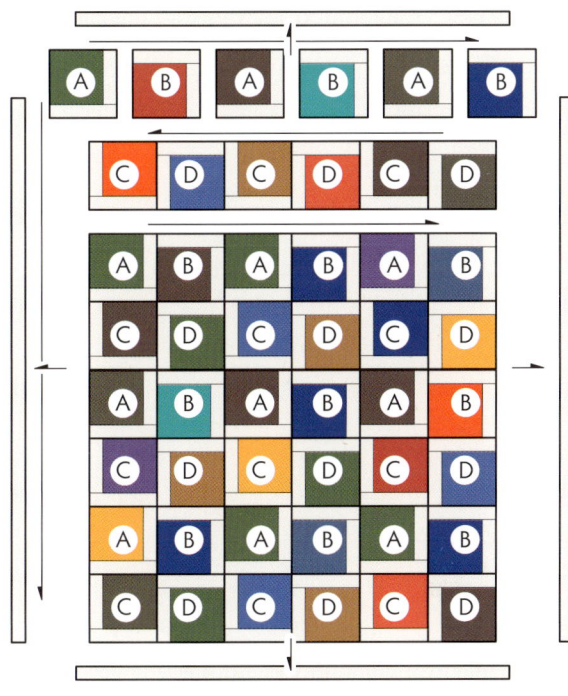

Quilt assembly

FINISHING THE QUILT

For more help on any of the finishing techniques, go to ShopMartingale.com for free downloadable information.

1. Layer the backing, batting, and quilt top; baste.

2. Quilt as desired. I quilted an overall footballs-and-loops design.

3. Bind the quilt using the blue 2¼"-wide strips (see "Binding" on page 10).

THE WINNING STRATEGY

Finished quilt: 54½" x 62½" | Finished block: 8" x 8" | Skill level: Intermediate

MATERIALS

Yardage is based on 42"-wide fabric.

2 yards of red print for blocks, border, and binding

1 yard of cream print for blocks

1 yard of sport-theme print for blocks*

1 yard of red-and-white print for blocks*

3⅜ yards of backing fabric

61" x 69" piece of batting

*If your fabric is 60" wide, you'll need ¾ yard.

CUTTING

From the red print, cut:

    6 strips, 5¼" x 42"; crosscut into 42 squares, 5¼" x 5¼". Cut each square into quarters diagonally to yield 168 triangles.

    6 strips, 3½" x 42"

    6 strips, 2¼" x 42"

From the cream print, cut:

    6 strips, 5¼" x 42"; crosscut into 42 squares, 5¼" x 5¼". Cut each square into quarters diagonally to yield 168 triangles.

From the sport-theme print, cut:

    21 squares on the diagonal, 6¼" x 6¼"*

From the red-and-white print, cut:

    21 squares on the diagonal, 6¼" x 6¼"*

*See "Cutting on the Diagonal" (page 8) for cutting sports-logo prints at a 45° angle.

PIECING BLOCK A

1 Sew a cream 5¼" triangle to a red 5¼" triangle side by side as shown. Make 42 of these units with the red triangle on the right and 42 with the red triangle on the left.

Make 42 of each.

2 Sew pieced triangles from step 1 to opposite sides of a red-and-white 6¼" square; make sure you orient them as shown. Press the seam allowances toward the square. Then sew pieced triangles to the remaining sides of the square. Press the seam allowances toward the triangles. The block should measure 8½" square. Repeat to make a total of 21 blocks.

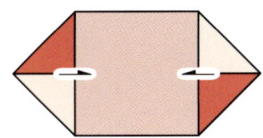

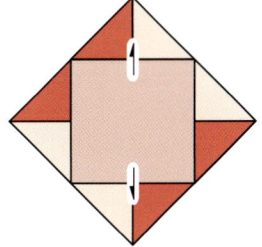 

Block A.
Make 21.

PIECING BLOCK B

1 Sew the remaining cream and red 5¼" triangles together, making sure that the red fabric is on the right. Press the seam allowances toward the red. Repeat to make a total of 84 units.

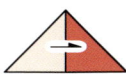

Make 84.

2 Sew the units to opposite sides of a sport-theme 6¼" square. Press the seam allowances toward the square. Sew two more triangle units to the remaining sides. Press the seam allowances toward the triangles. The block should measure 8½" square. Repeat to make a total of 21 blocks.

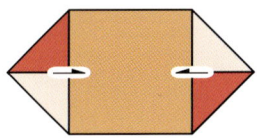

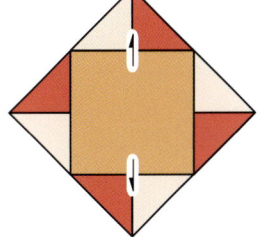 

Block B.
Make 21.

The Winning Strategy

ASSEMBLING THE QUILT TOP

1 Lay out the blocks according to the quilt assembly diagram below, alternating blocks A and B. Sew them into rows. Press the seam allowances in opposite directions from row to row. Sew the rows together and press the seam allowances in one direction.

2 Sew the red 3½"-wide strips together, end to end. Measure the quilt through the center from top to bottom and cut strips to that measurement. Sew the strips to the sides of the quilt top. Press the seam allowances toward the border strips.

3 Measure the quilt through the center from side to side, including the borders just added. Cut two strips to that length. Sew the trimmed strips to the top and bottom edges of the quilt top. Press the seam allowances toward the border strips.

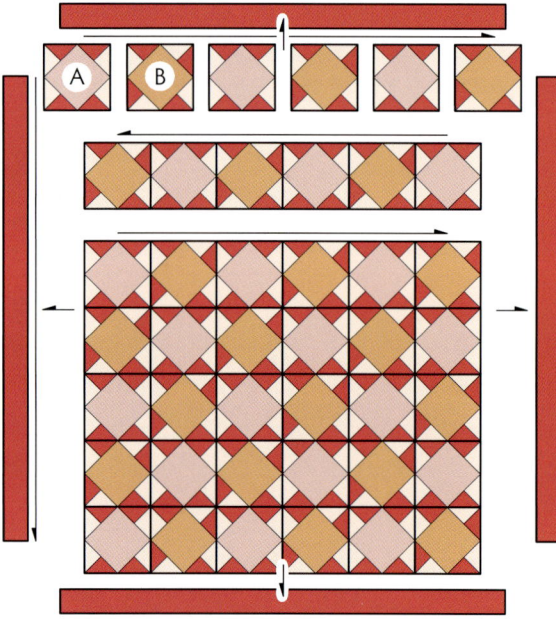

Quilt assembly

FINISHING THE QUILT

For more help on any of the finishing techniques, go to ShopMartingale.com for free downloadable information.

1 Layer the backing, batting, and quilt top; baste.

2 Quilt as desired. I quilted baseballs across the entire quilt.

3 Bind the quilt using the red 2¼"-wide strips (see "Binding" on page 10).

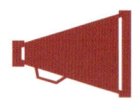 **Not Your Sport? Try This...**

GOING FOR OVERTIME

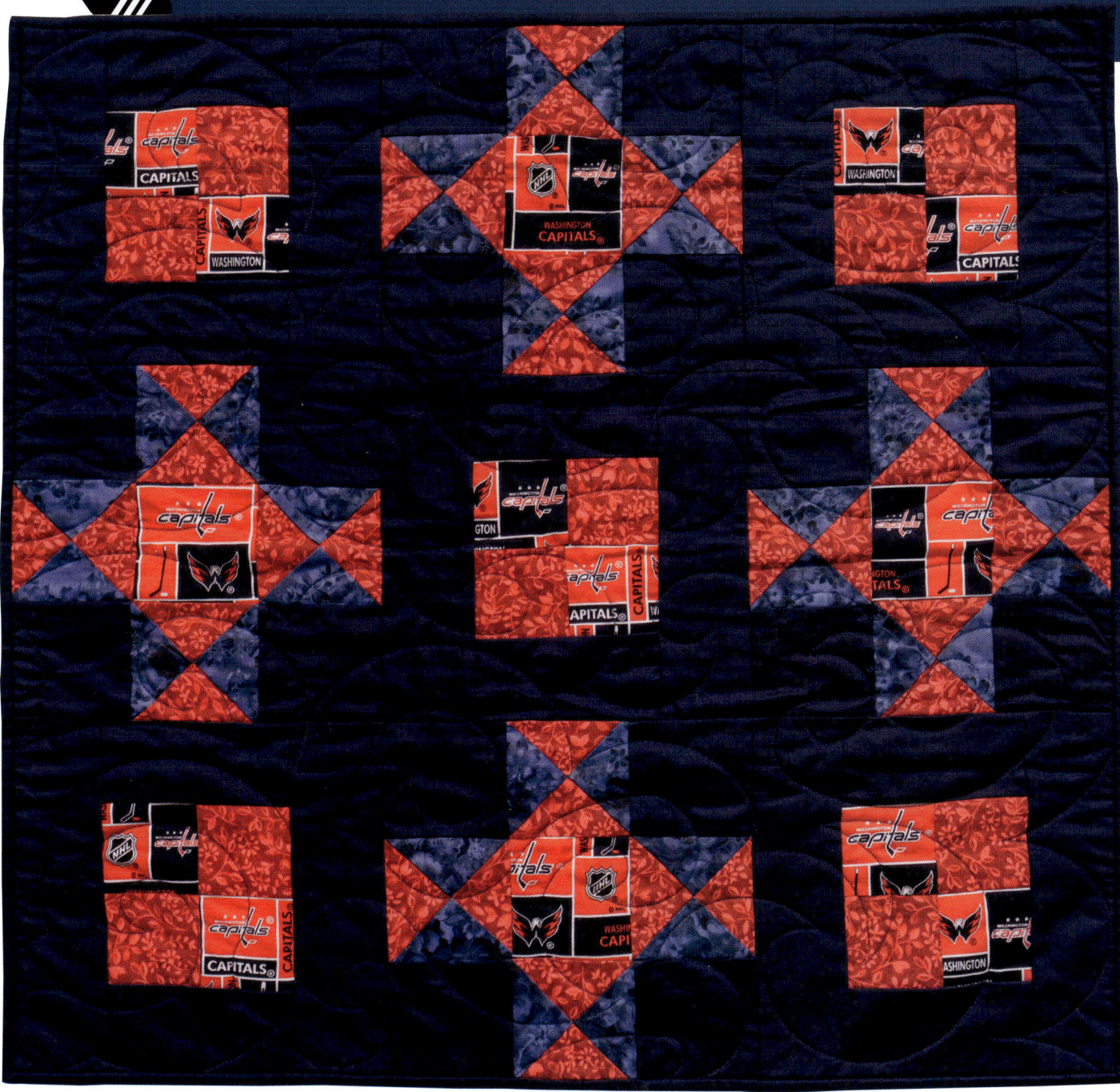

Finished quilt: 27½" x 27½" | Finished block: 9" x 9" | Skill level: Intermediate

43

MATERIALS

Yardage is based on 42"-wide fabric.

⅞ yard of navy solid for blocks and binding

½ yard of sport-logo print for blocks

¼ yard of red print for blocks

¼ yard of medium-blue print for blocks

1 yard of backing fabric

34" x 34" square of batting

CUTTING

From the navy solid, cut:

   1 strip, 5" x 42"; crosscut into 10 rectangles, 2¾" x 5"

   3 strips, 2¾" x 42"; crosscut into 10 rectangles, 2¾" x 9½"

   2 strips, 3½" x 42"; crosscut into 16 squares, 3½" x 3½"

   3 strips, 2¼" x 42"

From the sport-logo print, cut:

   1 strip, 3½" x 42"; crosscut into 4 squares, 3½" x 3½"

   1 strip, 2¾" x 42"; crosscut into 10 squares, 2¾" x 2¾"

From red print, cut:

   1 strip, 4¼" x 42"; crosscut into 8 squares, 4¼" x 4¼". Cut each square into quarters diagonally to yield 32 triangles.

   1 strip 2¾" x 42"; crosscut into 10 squares, 2¾" x 2¾"

From medium-blue print, cut:

   1 strip 4¼" x 42"; crosscut into 8 squares, 4¼" x 4¼". Cut each square into quarters diagonally to yield 32 triangles.

PIECING THE OHIO STAR BLOCKS

1 Sew the red 4¼" and the medium-blue 4¼" triangles together with the red triangles on the right. Press the seam allowances toward the medium-blue triangles. Make a total of 32.

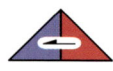

Make 32.

2 Sew two pieced triangle units together to make a quarter-square-triangle unit. Press the seam allowances to one side. The quarter-square-triangle unit should measure 3½" square. Make a total of 16.

Make 16.

3 Lay out four quarter-square-triangle units from step 2, four navy 3½" squares, and one sport-logo 3½" square as shown. Sew into rows and press as indicated by the arrows. Sew the rows together and press. The block should measure 9½" square. Repeat to make a total of four Ohio Star blocks.

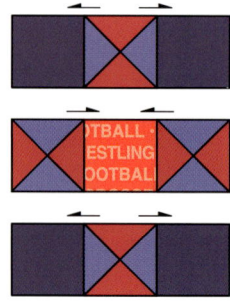 

Make 4.

PIECING THE BORDERED FOUR PATCH BLOCKS

1 Sew a red 2¾" square to a sport-logo 2¾" square. Press the seam allowances toward the red. Repeat to make a total of 10 units. Sew two units together and press as indicated by the arrows. The four-patch unit should measure 5" square. Repeat to make a total of five units, being careful to place the sport-logo print correctly.

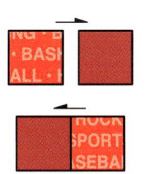 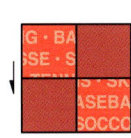

Make 5.

2 Sew navy 2¾" x 5" rectangles to the tops and bottoms of the units from step 1. Press the seam allowances toward the rectangles. Sew navy 2¾" x 9½" rectangles to the sides. Press the seam allowances toward the rectangles. The Bordered Four Patch blocks should measure 9½" square. Repeat to make five.

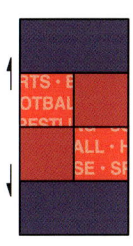 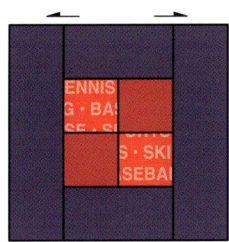

Make 5.

ASSEMBLING THE QUILT TOP

Lay out the blocks according to the quilt assembly diagram below, alternating the Ohio Star and the Bordered Four Patch blocks. Sew the blocks into rows and press in opposite directions from row to row. Join the rows and press in one direction.

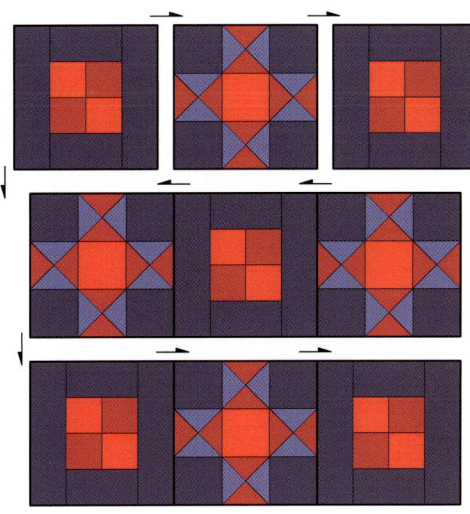

Quilt assembly

FINISHING THE QUILT

For more help on any of the finishing techniques, go to ShopMartingale.com for free downloadable information.

1 Layer the backing, batting, and quilt top; baste.

2 Quilt as desired. I quilted large overall waves.

3 Bind the quilt using the navy 2¼"-wide navy strips (see "Binding" on page 10).

Going For Overtime **45**

TAILGATING TABLE RUNNER

MATERIALS

Yardage is based on 42"-wide fabric unless otherwise noted.

1⅛ yards of sport-logo print*

1 yard of white print for setting triangles

½ yard of medium-blue solid for border

½ yard navy solid for binding

1½ yards of backing fabric

28" x 62" piece of batting

*If your fabric is 60"-wide, you'll need ⅝ yard.

CUTTING

From the sport-logo print, cut:

3 diagonal-cut squares, 12" x 12"

From the white print, cut:

1 square, 12½" x 12½", crosscut into quarters diagonally to yield 4 triangles

1 strip, 12½" x 42"; crosscut into 2 squares, 12½" x 12½". Cut each square in half diagonally to yield 4 triangles.

From the medium-blue solid, cut:

4 strips, 2½" x 42"

From the navy solid, cut:

4 strips, 2¼" x 42"

*See "Cutting on the Diagonal" (page 8) for cutting sport-logo prints at a 45°.

Finished quilt: 21½" x 55½"   Skill level: Beginner

ASSEMBLING THE RUNNER TOP

1. Lay out the sport-logo 12" squares and the large and small white triangles into diagonal rows as shown. Stitch the rows together and press the seam allowances as indicated by the arrows. Then join the rows and press.

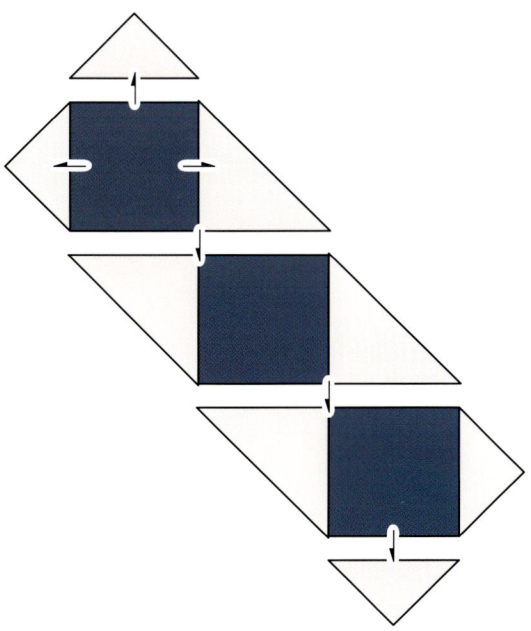

2. Join the medium-blue 2½"-wide strips together end to end. Measure the table runner through the center from top and bottom and cut strips to that measurement. Sew the strips to the long sides of the quilt top. Press the seam allowances toward the border strips.

3. Measure the table runner through the center from side to side, including the borders just added. Cut two strips to that measurement. Sew the trimmed strips to the ends of the table-runner top. Press the seam allowances toward the border strips.

FINISHING THE RUNNER

For more help on any of the finishing techniques, go to ShopMartingale.com for free downloadable information.

1. Layer the backing, batting, and quilt top; baste.

2. Quilt as desired. I quilted footballs and loops throughout.

3. Bind the quilt using the navy 2¼"-wide strips (see "Binding" on page 10).

 Bed-Runner Option

This pattern can be used to make a bed runner. Measure your bed across the bottom and add the amount of runner you want to hang over the sides. The 12" squares of sport-logo print measure about 17" across the diagonal, so divide the length you want by 17 to determine how many squares you'll need. For example, a queen-size bed is 60" across. If you'd like the runner to hang down 10" on each side, you'd like your runner to be 80" long. Divide 80" by 17 and you get 4.7. Round that up to 5 for a total of five sport-logo squares.

Bed size	Number of squares needed	Number of setting triangles needed	Finished length
Twin	4	6	72" long
Full	5	8	89" long
Queen	6	10	106" long
King	7	12	123" long

About the Author

I started sewing at age eight along with my two sisters. Our grandmother taught us on her Singer treadle machine and had all of us sewing up a storm within a short time. My love of sewing carried over into quilting when I grew up. Quilting has always been my stress reliever from my occupation in the field of radiology. I like to challenge myself, so I would alter quilt patterns to make them my own.

My quilt sisters found these altered patterns to be interesting and started asking me to change, redesign, and draft patterns to suit the focus fabrics they wanted to incorporate into their quilts. Eventually I started my own quilting business, Sew Bee It. I absolutely love coming up with quilting designs for quilts in order to give them that finishing touch. As the business grew, I began teaching quilting patterns and techniques, and decided to share my experiences by publishing.

Photo by J. Ward Poole

Acknowledgments

I'd like to thank my husband, Doug Olivieri, for supporting me while I pursue my dreams and do what I love. He has reinforced that I should do what my passion is, no matter what others may tell me.

Thanks to my quilt sister, Alesia Steinberger, who listened to me, provided reinforcement when needed, and assisted me with cutting and binding.

Thank you to a great friend, Ward Poole, who took beautiful photographs of these quilts for the submission of this book.

Members of my quilt guild, Friendship Quilt Guild of Linthicum, were all very encouraging throughout the book-writing process. It's through this "village" that this book came to fruition. Thank you!

A big thank-you to the staff at Martingale for their guidance and confidence. Since experiencing the learning process of publishing a book, I have come to appreciate their creative input along with their patience, encouragement, and education. *Team Spirit* has been an exciting journey and I look forward to more in the future.

What's your creative passion?
Find it at **ShopMartingale.com**
books • eBooks • ePatterns • daily blog • free projects
videos • tutorials • inspiration • giveaways